Jesus Said That...

&

So Much More...

shELAH

© 2019

Publisher: yOur BackYard
Centerville TN 37033
USA

Cover Design:	Clint Clarneau
Creative Consultant:	Randall Sandefur
Marketing Manager:	Erin Murphy Anderson
Editors:	B.J. Grainger

Preface

"I have to think about that...." This notable response from Tyler, one of my grandsons, encouraged me to think more about the word *that*. I had just asked Tyler, "What's your favorite Bible verse that shares something that Jesus said?" If someone had unexpectedly asked me my own question, I would also have likely needed time to think.

Reassuring words that Jesus Christ said, recorded in John 3:17, that God did not send Him, Jesus to condemn us, but to save those who believe in Him, comfort me. Believing in Jesus and trusting His Words frees and enlivens us.

Tyler's response encouraged me to complete *Jesus Said That....* I pray this book, which correlates Words Jesus said (in English, عربي & Española) with diverse traffic signs will encourage readers to not only read but also heed them—and get to know Him. Thinking about the fact Jesus came so we may have eternal life; that we may know Him, amazes me.

The good news that Jesus, God's only begotten Son, died on the cross to free us from the penalty of sin; to secure eternal life for those who "believe in Him" amazes me. The fact that He lives today and calls us to trust Him; to be "born again;" to have a personal relationship with Him amazes me.

Our new birth brings us into the family that calls God, "Father." Even though Jesus no longer physically lives with us on this side of Heaven, He did not abandon us when He returned to His Heavenly home. Just as Jesus promised (recorded in John 14), He sent the Holy Spirit to comfort and guide those who believe in Him. He left us His Words. Jesus, "the Way, the Truth and the Life," gives eternal life... to "whosoever" believes in Him.

Jesus Said That...

Socrates taught for 40 years. Plato for 50, Aristotle for 40, and Jesus for only 3. Yet the influence of Christ's 3-year ministry infinitely transcends the impact left by the combined 130 years of teaching from these men who were among the greatest philosophers of all antiquity.
~ Unknown

Buddha never claimed to be God. Moses never claimed to be Jehovah. Mohammed never claimed to be Allah. Yet Jesus Christ claimed to be the true and living God. Buddha simply said, "I am a teacher in search of the truth." Jesus said, "I am the Truth." Confucius said, "I never claimed to be holy." Jesus said, "Who convicts me of sin?" Mohammed said, "Unless God throws his cloak of mercy over me, I have no hope." Jesus said, "Unless you believe in me, you will die in your sins." ~ Unknown

A man who was merely a man and said the sort of things Jesus said would not be a great moral teacher. He would either be a lunatic—on a level with the man who says he is a poached egg—or else he would be the Devil of Hell. You must make your choice. Either this man was, and is, the Son of God; or else a madman or something worse. You can shut Him up for a fool, you can spit at Him and kill Him as a demon; or you can fall at His feet and call Him Lord and God. But let us not come with any patronizing nonsense about His being a great human teacher. He has not left that open to us. He did not intend to. ~ C.S. Lewis

Signs

Who do you say?..1
One Way..3
Yield..5
Can't Serve Both..7
Love..9
Work..11
Stop...13
Rest...15
Wrong Way...17
Watch & Pray...19
Faith Ahead...21
U-Turn Allowed..23
Gospel Info...25
Dead End..27
Safety Info...29
Warning..31
Final Exit..33
Coming Soon..35

One Solitary Life

Here is a man who was born in an obscure village, the Child of a peasant woman. He worked in a carpenter shop until He was thirty, and then for three years He was an itinerant preacher. He never wrote a book. He never held an office.

He never owned a home. He never had a family. He never went to college. He never put His foot inside a big city. He never traveled two hundred miles from the place where He was born. He never did one of the things that usually accompany greatness. He had no credentials but Himself. He had nothing to do with this world except the naked power of His Divine manhood. While still a young man, the tide of popular opinion turned against Him. He was turned over to His enemies. He went through the mockery of a trial.

He was nailed to a Cross between two thieves.

His executioners gambled for the only piece of property He had on earth while He was dying—and that was His coat. When He was dead He was taken down and laid in a borrowed grave through the pity of a friend. Such was His human life—*He rises from the dead.*

Nineteen wide centuries have come and gone and today He is the Centerpiece of the human race and the Leader of the column of progress. I am within the mark when I say that all the armies that ever marched, and all the navies that ever were built, and all the parliaments that ever sat, and all the kings that ever reigned, put together, have not affected the life of man upon this earth as powerfully as has that "One Solitary Life."

~ James C. Hefley*

*Inspired by an essay James A. Francis wrote and then used during a 1926 sermon.

Matthew 6:9-13
New King James Version (NKJV)

Our Father in heaven,
Hallowed be Your name.
Your kingdom come.
Your will be done
On earth as it is in heaven.
Give us this day our daily bread.
And forgive us our debts,
As we forgive our debtors.
And do not lead us into temptation,
But deliver us from the evil one. For
Yours is the kingdom
and the power
and the glory
forever.
Amen.

متى 9:6-13

9 لِذَلِكَ صَلُّوا كَما يَلي:

‹أبانا الَّذي في السَّماءِ،
لِيَتَقَدَّس اسْمُك،
10 لِيَأْتِ مَلَكوتُك،
فَتَكونَ مَشيئَتُك،
هُنا عَلى الأرْضِ كَما هِيَ في السَّماءِ.
11 أعطِنا اليَوْمَ خُبزَنا كَفافَ يَوْمِنا،
12 واغفِرْ لَنا خَطايانا،
كَما غَفَرْنا نَحنُ أيضاً لِلَّذينَ يُسيئونَ إلَينا.
13 ولا تُدْخِلْنا في تَجرِبَةٍ،
بَلْ أنقِذْنا مِنَ الشِّرِّيرِ. [a]
لأنَّ لَكَ المُلْكَ والقُدرَةَ والمَجدَ،
إلى أبَدِ الآبدينَ. آمين›

Footnotes:

a. متى 6:13/*الشِّرِّير*. الشَّيطان (إبليس).

Mateo 6:9-13
Spanish Blue Red and Gold Letter Edition
(SRV-BRG)

Vosotros pues, oraréis así:
Padre nuestro que estás en los cielos,
antificado sea tu nombre.
Venga tu reino.
Sea hecha tu voluntad,
como en el cielo,
así también en la tierra.
Danos hoy nuestro pan cotidiano.
Y perdónanos nuestras deudas, como
también nosotros perdonamos á
nuestros deudores.
Y no nos metas en tentación,
mas líbranos del mal:
porque tuyo es el reino,
y el poder,
y la gloria, por todos
los siglos.
Amén.

Only through repentance and faith
in Christ
can anyone be saved.
No religious activity will be sufficient,
only true faith in Jesus Christ alone.
~ Ravi Zacharias

Comparison of Things God & Jesus Said....

And God said to Moses, "I AM WHO I AM." And He said, "Thus you shall say to the children of Israel, 'I AM has sent me to you.'"
~ Exodus 3:14

Jesus said to them, "Most assuredly, I say to you, before Abraham was, I AM."
~ John 8:58

So He [God] drove out the man [Adam]; and He placed cherubim at the east of the garden of Eden, and a flaming sword which turned every way, to guard the way to the tree of life.
~ Genesis 3:24

I am the way, the truth, and the life. No one comes to the Father except through Me.
~ John 14:6

I am He, I am the First, I am also the Last.
~ Isaiah 48:12

I am the Alpha and the Omega, the Beginning and the End, the First and the Last.
~ Revelation 22:13

Matthew

WHEN JESUS CAME into the region of Caesarea Philippi, He asked His disciples, saying, "Who do men say that I, the Son of Man, am?" So they said, "Some say John the Baptist, some Elijah, and others Jeremiah or one of the prophets."

He said to them,

"But who do you say that I am?"
Simon Peter answered and said,
"You are the Christ, the Son of the living God."
~ Matthew 16:13–16

متى 16:13-16

بُطرُسُ يُعلِنُ أنَ يَسُوعَ هُوَ المَسِيح

13 وَعِندَما أتَى يَسُوعُ إلَى إقلِيمِ قَيصَرِيَّةِ فِيلِبُّسَ، سألَ تَلامِيذَهُ: «مَنْ يَقُولُ النّاسُ إنِّي أنا، ابْنَ الإنسانِ؟»

14 فَأجابَ تَلامِيذُهُ: «بَعضُهُمْ يَقُولُ إنَّكَ يُوحَنّا المَعْمَدانُ، وآخَرُونَ إنَّكَ إيلِيّا، وآخَرُونَ إنَّكَ إرمِيا، أوْ نَبِيٌّ كَباقِي الأنبِياءِ.»

15 فَقالَ لَهُمْ: «وَأنتُمْ، مَنْ أنا فِي رَأيِكُمْ؟»

16 فَأجابَ سِمعانُ بُطرُسُ: «أنتَ هُوَ المَسِيحُ، ابْنُ اللهِ الحَيِّ.»

13 Y viniendo Jesús á las partes de Cesarea de Filipo, preguntó á sus discípulos, diciendo: ¿Quién dicen los hombres que es el Hijo del hombre?
14 Y ellos dijeron: Unos, Juan el Bautista; y otros, Elías; y otros; Jeremías, ó alguno de los profetas.
15 El les dice: Y vosotros, ¿quién decís que soy?
16 Y respondiendo Simón Pedro, dijo: Tú eres el Cristo, el ijo del Dios viviente.

~ Mateo 16

**But
who do you
say that I am?**

~ Jesus asked that...

John

THOMAS SAID TO Him, "Lord, we do not know where You are going, and how can we know the way?" Jesus said to him,

I am the way, the truth,
and the life.
No one comes to the Father
except through Me.

~ John 14:5–6

يوحنا 5:14-6

5 فقَالَ لَهُ تُوما: «نَحنُ لا نَعرفُ إلى أَينَ أنتَ ذاهِبٌ يا رَبُّ! فَكَيفَ يُمكِنُنا أَنْ نَعرفَ الطَّريقَ»؟

6 فقَالَ لَهُ يَسُوعُ: «أنا هُوَ الطَّريقُ والحَقُّ والحَياةُ. لا أحَدَ يَأْتِي إلى الآبِ إلّا بِي.

5 Dícele Tomás: Señor, no sabemos á dónde vas: ¿cómo, pues, podemos saber el camino? 6 Jesús le dice:

Yo soy el camino,
y la verdad, y la vida:
nadie viene al Padre,
sino por mí.

~ Juan 14

I am the way, the truth, and the life.
No one comes to the Father except through Me.
~ Jesus said that...

John

THERE WAS A man of the Pharisees named Nicodemus, a ruler of the Jews (verse 1). ... Jesus answered and said to him, "Most assuredly, I say to you, unless one is born again, he cannot see the kingdom of God"

~ John 3:2–3

For God so loved the world that He gave His only begotten Son, that whoever believes in Him should not perish but have everlasting life. For God did not send His Son into the world to condemn the world, but that the world through Him

يوحنا 2:3-3

2 فجاء إلى يَسُوع ليلاً وقال لَهُ: «يا مُعلِّمُ، نَحْنُ نَعلَمُ أنَّكَ مُعلِّمٌ جِئتَ مِن عِندِ اللهِ، لأنَّهُ ما مِن أحَدٍ يَستَطيعُ أن يَصنَعَ المُعجِزاتِ الّتي تَصنَعُها أنتَ إن لَم يَكُنِ اللهُ مَعَهُ.»

3 فأجابَهُ يَسُوعُ: «أقُولُ الحَقَّ لَك: لَن يَرَى أحَدٌ مَلَكُوتَ اللهِ ما لَم يُولَدْ ثانِيَةً.»

يوحنا 3:16-17

16 فقَدْ أحَبَّ اللهُ العالَمَ كَثيراً، حَتَّى إنَّهُ قَدَّمَ ابنَهُ الوَحيدَ، لِكَيْ لا يَهلِكَ كُلُّ مَن يُؤمِنُ بِهِ، بَل تَكُونُ لَهُ الحَياةُ الأبَدِيَّةُ.

17 فاللهُ لَم يُرْسِلِ ابنَهُ إلى العالَمِ لِكَيْ يَدينَ العالَمَ، لَكِنَّهُ أرسَلَهُ لِكَيْ يُخَلِّصَ بِهِ العالَمَ.

Y HABÍA un hombre de los Fariseos que se llamaba Nicodemo, príncipe de los Judíos. ...3 Respondió Jesús, y díjole: De cierto, de cierto te digo, que el que no naciere otra vez, no puede ver el reino de Dios....

16 Porque de tal manera amó Dios al mundo, que ha dado á su Hijo unigénito, para que todo aquel que en él cree, no se pierda, mas tenga vida eterna. 17 Porque no envió Dios á su Hijo al mundo, para que condene al mundo, mas para que el mundo sea salvo por él.

~ Juan 3

For God so loved the world
that He gave His only begotten Son,
that whoever believes in Him should
not perish
but have everlasting life.

For God did not send His Son
into the world
to condemn the world,
but that the world
through Him
might be saved.
~ Jesus said that...

Luke

AND IF YOU have not been faithful in what is another man's, who will give you what is your own? 13 "No servant can serve two masters; for either he will hate the one and love the other, or else he will be loyal to the one and despise the other. You cannot serve God and mammon."

Now the Pharisees, who were lovers of money, also heard all these things, and they derided Him.

~ Luke 16:12–14

لوقا 12:16-14

12 وَإِنْ لَمْ تَكُونُوا أُمَناءَ فِي ما يَخُصُّ غَيرَكُمْ، فَمَنِ الَّذِي سَيُعطِيكُمْ ما يَخُصُّكُمْ؟

13 «لا يُمكِنُ لِخادِمٍ أَنْ يَخدِمَ سَيِّدَيْنِ. فَإِمّا أَنْ يَكرَهَ أَحَدَهُما وَيُحِبُّ الآخَرَ، وَإِمّا أَنْ يُخلِصَ لِأَحَدِهِما وَيَحتَقِرُ الآخَرَ. لا يُمكِنُكُمْ أَنْ تَخدِمُوا اللهَ وَالغِنَى.»

شَرِيعَةُ اللهِ لا تَتَغَيَّر

14 وَلَمّا سَمِعَ الفِرِّيسِيُّونَ هَذا كُلَّهُ، اسْتَهزَأُوا بِهِ لِأَنَّهُمْ كانُوا يُحِبُّونَ المالَ.

12 Y si en lo ajeno no fuisteis fieles, ¿quién os dará lo que es vuestro? 13 Ningún siervo puede servir á dos señores; porque ó aborrecerá al uno y amará al otro, ó se allegará al uno y menospreciará al otro. No podéis servir á Dios y á las riquezas.

14 Y oían también todas estas cosas los Fariseos, los cuales eran avaros, y se burlaban de él.

~ Lucas 16

No servant can serve two masters;
for either he will hate the one
and love the other,
or else
he will be loyal to the one
and despise the other.
You cannot serve God and mammon.*

~ Jesus said that...

*riches (when personified and opposed to God)

Matthew

THEN ONE OF them, a lawyer, asked Him a question, testing Him, and saying, "Teacher, which is the great commandment in the law?" Jesus said to him,

'You shall love the Lord your God
with all your heart,
with all your soul, and with all your mind.'

This is the first and great commandment.
And the second is like it:
'You shall love your neighbor as yourself.'
On these two commandments
hang all the Law and the Prophets.'"
~ Matthew 22:35–40

متى 22:35-40

35 وَسَأَلَهُ خَبِيرٌ فِي الشَّرِيعَةِ مُحَاوِلاً الإِيقَاعَ بِهِ فَقَالَ: 36 «يَا مُعَلِّمُ، مَا هِيَ أَعظَمُ وَصِيَّةٍ فِي الشَّرِيعَةِ؟»

37 فَقَالَ لَهُ يَسُوعُ: «‹تُحِبُّ الرَّبَّ إِلَهَكَ بِكُلِّ قَلبِكَ، وَبِكُلِّ نَفسِكَ، وَبِكُلِّ عَقلِكَ،› [a] 38 هَذِهِ هِيَ الوَصِيَّةُ الأُولَى وَالعُظمَى، 39 أَمَّا الوَصِيَّةُ الثَّانِيَةُ فَهِيَ كَالأُولَى: ‹تُحِبُّ صَاحِبَكَ [b] كَمَا تُحِبُّ نَفسَكَ.› [c] 40 الشَّرِيعَةُ كُلُّها وَكُتُبُ الأَنبِياءِ تَتَعَلَّقُ بِهَاتَينِ الوَصِيَّتَينِ.»

35 Y preguntó uno de ellos, intérprete de la ley, tentándole y diciendo: 36 Maestro, ¿cuál es el mandamiento grande en la ley? 37 Y Jesús le dijo:

Amarás al Señor tu Dios de todo tu
corazón, y de toda tu alma, y de toda tu mente. 38 Este es el primero y el grande mandamiento. 39 Y el segundo es semejante á éste: Amarás á tu prójimo como á ti mismo. 40 De estos dos mandamientos depende toda la ley y los profetas.
~ Mateo 22

You shall love the Lord your God
with all your heart, with all your soul,
and with all your mind.
...You shall love your neighbor
as yourself.
~ Jesus said that....

John

I must work the works
of Him who sent Me
while it is day;
the night is coming
when no one can work.
~ John 9:4

"Most assuredly, I say to you,
he who believes in Me,
the works that I do he will do also;
and greater works than these he will do,
because I go to My Father .
~ John 14:12

يوحنا 9:4
4 يَنبَغِي أَنْ نَعْمَلَ أعمالَ الّذي أرْسَلَني مادامَ الوَقْتُ نَهاراً. فَعِندَما يَأتي الّليلُ، لا يَسْتَطِيعُ أحَدُ أنْ يَعْمَلَ.

يوحنا 14:12 .
12 أقُولُ الحَقَّ لكُمْ: مَنْ يُؤمِنُ بِي، سَيَعمَلُ أيضاً الأعمالَ الّتي أعمَلُها أنا، بَلْ وسَيَعمَلُ أعظَمَ مِنها لأنّي ذاهِبٌ إلى الآبِ.

Conviéneme obrar las obras del que me envió,
entre tanto que el día dura:
la noche viene, cuando nadie puede obrar.
~ Juan 9:4
De cierto, de cierto os digo:
El que en mí cree,
as obras que yo hago también él las hará;
y mayores que éstas hará;
porque yo voy al Padre. ~
Juan 14:12

**I must work the works of Him who sent Me while it is day;
the night is coming when no one can work.**

**...I say to you, he who believes in Me,
the works that I do he will do also;
and greater works than these he will do,
because I go to My Father.**
~ **Jesus Said** that...

John

The Jews then complained about Him, because He said, "I am the bread which came down from heaven." And they said, "Is not this Jesus, the son of Joseph, whose father and mother we know? How is it then that He says, 'I have come down from heaven'?"

Jesus therefore answered and said to them,
Do not murmur among yourselves.
No one can come to Me
unless the Father who sent Me draws him;
and I will raise him up at the last day..
~ John 6:41–44

يوحنا 41:6-44

41 فَبَدَأ الْيَهودُ يَتَذَمَّرُونَ مِنْهُ لِأَنَّهُ قَالَ: «أَنَا هُوَ الْخُبْزُ الَّذِي نَزَلَ مِنَ السَّمَاءِ». 42 وَقَالُوا: «أَلَيْسَ هَذَا يَسُوعَ بْنَ يُوسُفَ؟ أَلَا نَعْرِفُ أَبَاهُ وَأُمَّهُ؟ فَكَيْفَ يَقُولُ الآنَ إِنَّهُ نَزَلَ مِنَ السَّمَاءِ؟»

43 فَأَجَابَهُمْ يَسُوعُ: «كَفَى تَذَمُّراً فِيمَا بَيْنَكُمْ. 44 لَا يُمْكِنُ لِأَحَدٍ أَنْ يَأْتِيَ إِلَيَّ إِنْ لَمْ يَجْذِبْهُ إِلَيَّ الآبُ الَّذِي أَرْسَلَنِي. وَفِي الْيَوْمِ الْأَخِيرِ، أَنَا سَأُقِيمُهُ.

41 Murmuraban entonces de él los Judíos, porque había dicho: Yo soy el pan que descendí del cielo.
42 Y decían: ¿No es éste Jesús, el hijo de José, cuyo padre y madre nosotros conocemos? ¿cómo, pues, dice éste: Del cielo he descendido?
43 Y Jesús respondió, y díjoles: No urmuréis entre vosotros.
44 Ninguno puede venir á mí,
si el Padre que me envió no le trajere;
y yo le resucitaré en el día postrero.
~ Juan 6

[Stop]
Do not
murmur among yourselves.
~ Jesus said that...

Mark & Matthew

Then the apostles gathered to Jesus and told Him all things, both what they had done and what they had taught. 31 And He said to them, "Come aside by yourselves to a deserted place and rest a while." For there were many coming and going, and they did not even have time to eat.

~ Mark 6:30–31

Come to Me, all you who labor and are heavy laden, and I will give you rest.

~ Matthew 11:28

مرقس 6:30-31

يَسُوعُ يُطعِمُ خَمسَةَ الآفِ شَخصٍ

30 وَاجتَمَعَ الرُسُلُ حَولَ يَسُوعَ وَأخبَرُوهُ عَن كُلِّ ما عَمِلُوهُ وَعَلَّموهُ. 31 فَقالَ لَهُمْ: «تَعالُوا لِنَذْهَبَ وَحدَنا إلَى مَكانٍ مُنْعَزِلٍ، وَنَستَرِيحَ قَلِيلاً.» هَذا لِأنَّ كَثِيرِينَ كانُوا يَأتُونَ وَيَذْهَبُونَ، فَلَمْ تَسنَحْ لَهُمْ فُرصَةٌ حَتَّى لِلأكلِ.

متى 11:28

28 «تَعالُوا إلَيَّ أيُّها المُتعَبِينَ وَيا مَنْ تَحمِلُونَ أحمالاً ثَقِيلَةً، وَأنا سَأعطِيكُمُ الرَّاحَةَ.

30 Y los apóstoles se juntaron con Jesús, y
le contaron todo lo que habían hecho,
y lo que habían enseñado.
31 Y él les dijo: Venid vosotros aparte al lugar desierto,
y reposad un poco.
Porque eran muchos los que iban y venían,
que ni aun tenían lugar de comer.

~ Marcos 6:30–31

28 Venid á mí todos los que estáis trabajados y cargados,
que yo os haré descansar.

~ Mateo 11:28

Come aside by yourselves
to a deserted place and
rest a while.

Come to Me,
all you who labor and are heavy
laden, and I will give you rest.
~ **Jesus said** that...

Matthew

Therefore I say to you, do not worry about your life, what you will eat or what you will drink; nor about your body, what you will put on. Is not life more than food and the body more than clothing? Look at the birds of the air, for they neither sow nor reap nor gather into barns; yet your heavenly Father feeds them. Are you not of more value than they? Which of you by worrying can add one cubit to his stature?

~ Matthew 6:25–27

متى 6:25-27

مَلَكُوتُ اللهِ أَوَّلاً

25 »لِهذا أَقُولُ لكُم، لا تَقلَقُوا مِن جِهةِ مَعيشَتِكُم، أيْ بِشَأنِ ما سَتَأكُلُونَ وَتَشرَبُونَ. وَلا تَقلَقُوا مِنْ جِهةِ جَسَدِكُم، أيْ بِشَأنِ ما سَتَلبَسُونَ. لِأنَّ الحَياةَ أكثَرُ أَهَمّيّةً مِنَ الطَّعامِ، وَالجَسَدَ أكثَرُ أَهَمّيّةً مِنَ اللِّباسِ. 26 انظُرُوا طُيُورَ السَّماءِ، فَهيَ لا تَبذُرُ وَلا تَحصُدُ، وَلا تَجمَعُ القَمحَ فِي مَخازِنَ، وَأبُوكُمُ السَّماوِيُّ يُطعِمُها. أَلَستُمْ أَثمَنَ عِندَ اللهِ مِنَ الطُّيورِ؟ 27 مَنْ مِنكُم يَستَطِيعُ أَنْ يُضِيفَ إلى عُمرِهِ ساعَةً واحِدَةً عِندَما يَقلَقُ؟

25 Por tanto os digo: No os congojéis por vuestra vida, qué habéis de comer, ó que habéis de beber; ni por vuestro cuerpo, qué habéis de vestir: ¿no es la vida más que el alimento, y el cuerpo que el vestido? 26 Mirad las aves del cielo, que no siembran, ni siegan, ni allegan en alfolíes; y vuestro Padre celestial las alimenta. ¿No sois vosotros mucho mejores que ellas? 27 Mas ¿quién de vosotros podrá, congojándose, añadir á su estatura un codo?

~ Mateo 6

Therefore don't worry about tomorrow,
because tomorrow will worry about itself.
Each day has enough trouble of its own.
~ Jesus said that...

Matthew

THEN HE CAME to the disciples and found them sleeping, and said to Peter,

What! Could you not watch with Me one hour?
Watch and pray,
lest you enter into temptation.
The spirit indeed is willing,
but the flesh is weak.

~ Matthew 26:40–41

متى 40:26-41

40 وَجاءَ إلى تَلامِيذِهِ، فَوَجَدَهُمْ نائِمِينَ، فَقالَ لِبُطرُسَ: «أهَكَذا لَمْ تَقدِرُوا أنْ تَسهَرُوا مَعِي ساعَةً واحِدَةً؟ **41** اسْهَرُوا وَصَلُّوا لِكَي لا تُجَرَّبُوا. رُوحُكُمْ تَسعَى إلَى ذَلِكَ، أمّا جَسَدُكُمْ فَضَعِيفٌ.»

40 Y vino á sus discípulos, y los halló durmiendo, y dijo á Pedro:

¿Así no habéis podido velar conmigo una hora? 41 Velad y orad,
para que no entréis en tentación:
el espíritu á la verdad está presto,
mas la carne enferma.
~ Mateo 26

Watch* and pray,
lest you enter into temptation.
The spirit indeed is willing,
but the flesh is weak.

~ Jesus said that...

* pay rigorous attention to, be active, cautious...

Luke

BUT HE SAID to them, "Where is your faith?" And they were afraid, and marveled, saying to one another, "Who can this be? For He commands even the winds and water, and they obey Him!"

~ Luke 8:25

And the apostles said to the Lord, "Increase our faith." So the Lord said,

"If you have faith as a mustard seed,
you can say to this mulberry tree,
'Be pulled up by the roots and be planted in the sea,'
and it would obey you.

~ Luke 17:5–6

لوقا 8:25

25 فَقَالَ يَسُوعُ لَهُمْ: «أينَ إيمانُكُمْ؟» لَكِنَّهُمْ كانُوا خائِفِينَ وَمَذهُولِينَ، وَهُمْ يَقُولونَ بَعضُهُمْ لِبَعضٍ: «أيُّ رَجُلٍ هَذا الَّذي يَأمُرُ الرّيحَ والمِياهَ، فَيُطِيعانِهِ؟»

لوقا 17:5-6

قَوَةُ الإيمان

5 وَقالَ الرُّسُلُ لِلرَّبِّ: «قَوِّ إيمانَنا.»

6 فَقالَ الرَّبُّ: «لَوْ كانَ إيمانُكُم فِي حَجمِ بِذْرَةِ الخَردَلِ، لَأمكَنَكُم أن تَأمُرُوا شَجَرَةَ التُّوتِ هَذِهِ فَتَقولوا لَها: ‹انقَلِعِي وَانزَرِعِي فِي البَحرِ،›، فَتُطِيعَكُم.»

25 Y les dijo: ¿Qué es de vuestra fe? Y atemorizados, se maravillaban, diciendo los unos á los otros: ¿Quién es éste, que aun á los vientos y al agua manda, y le obedecen?

~ Lucas 8

5 Y dijeron los apóstoles al Señor: Auméntanos la fe. 6 Entonces el Señor dijo: Si tuvieseis fe como un grano de mostaza, diréis á este sicómoro: Desarráigate, y plántate en el mar; y os obedecerá.

~ Lucas 17

Where is your faith?
    ~ Jesus said that...

Matthew

THEREFORE IF YOU bring your gift to the altar
and there remember that your brother
has something against you,
leave your gift there before the altar,
and go your way.
First be reconciled to your brother,
and then come and offer your gift.
~ Matthew 5:23–24

متى 5:23-24

23 »لِذلِكَ إنْ كُنتَ تُقَدِّمُ تَقدِمَةً عَلى المَذْبَحِ، وَهُناكَ تَذَكَّرْتَ أنَّ شَخصاً آخَرَ لَهُ شَيءٌ عَلَيكَ، 24 فَاترُكْ تَقدِمَتَكَ هُناكَ أمامَ المَذْبَحِ، وَاذْهَبْ وَاصْطَلِحْ مَعَ ذَلِكَ الشَّخصِ أوَّلاً، ثُمَّ ارجِعْ وَقَدِّمْ تَقدِمَتَكَ.

23 Por tanto, si trajeres tu presente al altar,
y allí te acordares de que tu hermano
tiene algo contra ti,
24 Deja allí tu presente delante del altar, y
vete, vuelve primero en amistad con tu hermano,
y entonces ven y ofrece tu presente. ~
Mateo 5

First be reconciled to your brother,
and
then come and offer your gift [to God].

~ Jesus said that...

Luke

THEN HE SAID to them,
Thus it is written,
and thus it was necessary for the Christ to suffer
and to rise from the dead the third day,
and that repentance and remission of sins
should be preached in His name to all nations,
beginning at Jerusalem.
And you are witnesses of these things.
~ Luke 24:46 -48

لوقا 46:24-48

46 وَقالَ لَهُمْ: «نَعَمْ، مَكتُوبٌ أَنَّ المَسِيحَ لا بُدَّ أَنْ يَتَأَلَّمَ وَيَقُومَ مِنَ المَوتِ فِي اليَومِ الثَّالِثِ. **47** وَلا بُدَّ أَنْ يُبَشَّرَ بِالتَّوبَةِ وَمَغفِرَةِ الخَطايا بِاسْمِهِ لِجَمِيعِ الأُمَمِ ابتِداءً مِنَ مَدِينَةِ القُدْسِ. **48** وَأَنتُمْ شُهُودٌ عَلَى تِلكَ الأُمُورِ.

46 Y díjoles: Así está escrito, y
así fué necesario
que el Cristo padeciese, y resucitase
de los muertos al tercer día;
47 Y que se predicase en su nombre el
arrepentimiento y la remisión de pecados
en todas las naciones,
comenzando de Jerusalem.
48 Y vosotros sois testigos de estas cosas.
~ Lucas 24

...it was necessary for the Christ
to suffer [and die on the cross]
and
to rise from the dead the third day,
and that repentance
and remission of sins
should be preached
in His name to all nations,
~ Jesus said that...

Luke

MY FRIENDS, LISTEN to me. Don't be afraid of those who kill the body but can't do any more than that. I will show you whom you should be afraid of. Be afraid of the one who has the authority to throw you into hell after you have been killed. Yes, I tell you, be afraid of him. Aren't five sparrows sold for two pennies? But God does not forget even one of them. In fact, he even counts every hair on your head! So don't be afraid. You are worth more than many sparrows.

لوقا 4:12-7

خافوا اللّٰهَ وَحدَه

4 «أقولُ لَكُم يا أحِبائي، لا تَخافوا مِنَ الّذينَ يَقتُلونَ الجَسَدَ، ثُمّ لا يَقدِرونَ أن يَفعَلوا ما هُوَ أكثَرُ. 5 سَأقولُ لَكُم مِمَّنْ يَنبَغي أن تَخافوا: خافوا مِنْ ذَلِكَ الّذي لَهُ السُّلطانُ أن يُلقِيَ في جُهنَّمَ بَعدَ أن يَقتُلَ. نَعَم، أقولُ لَكُم خافوا مِنهُ.

6 «أما تُباعُ خَمسَةُ عَصافيرَ بِفِرشَينِ؟ وَمَعَ ذَلِكَ، فإنّ اللّٰهَ لا يَنسَى واحِداً مِنها. 7 أمّا أنتُم فَحَتّى شَعرُ رَأسِكُم كُلُّهُ مَعدودٌ. فَلا تَخافوا، فأنتُم أثمَنُ مِنْ عَصافيرَ كَثيرَةٍ.

4 Mas os digo, amigos míos: No temáis de los que matan el cuerpo, y después no tienen más que hacer. 5 Mas os enseñaré á quién temáis: temed á aquel que después de haber quitado la vida, tiene poder de echar en la Gehenna: así os digo: á éste temed. 6 ¿No e venden cinco pajarillos por dos blancas? pues ni uno de ellos está olvidado delante de Dios. 7 Y aun los cabellos de vuestra cabeza están todos contados. No temáis pues: de más estima sois que muchos pajarillos.

~ Lucas 12

Don't be afraid of those
who kill the body
but can't do any more than that.

..He even counts
every hair on your head!
So don't be afraid.
You are worth more
than many sparrows.

~ Jesus said that...

John

THEN THE JEWS surrounded Him and said to Him, "How long do You keep us in doubt? If You are the Christ, tell us plainly." Jesus answered them,

"I told you, and you do not believe.
The works that I do in My Father's name,
they bear witness of Me.
But you do not believe, because you are not of My sheep,
as I said to you. My sheep hear My voice, and I know them,
and they follow Me. And I give them eternal life,
and they shall never perish;
neither shall anyone snatch them out of My hand...."
~ John 10: 24–28

يوحنا 10:24-28

24 فَأحاطَ بِهِ اليَهودُ وقالوا لَهُ: «حَتَّى مَتَى سَتُبْقِينا مُعَلَّقِينَ؟ إنْ كُنْتَ أنتَ المَسِيحَ، فَقُلْ لَنا صَراحَةً.»

25 أجابَهُمْ يَسُوعُ: «لَقَدْ قُلْتُ لَكُمْ وأنتُمْ تَرفُضُونَ أنْ تُصَدِّقُوا. الأعمالُ الَّتِي أعمَلُها بِاسْمِ أبِي تَشْهَدُ لِي. **26** لَكِنَّكُمْ تَرفُضُونَ أنْ تُصَدِّقُوا لِأنَّكُمْ لَسْتُمْ مِنْ خِرافِي. **27** فَخِرافِي تُصغِي إلَى صَوْتِي، وأنا أعرِفُها وهِيَ تَتبَعُنِي. **28** وأنا أعطِيها حَياةً أبَدِيَّةً ولَنْ تَهلِكَ أبَداً، ولَنْ يَنتَزِعَها أحَدٌ مِنْ يَدِي.

24 Y rodeáronle los Judíos y dijéronle: ¿Hasta cuándo nos has de turbar el alma? Si tú eres el Cristo, dínoslo abiertamente.

25 Respondióles Jesús: Os lo he dicho, y no creéis: las obras
que yo hago en nombre de mi Padre, ellas dan testimonio
de mí; 26 Mas vosotros no creéis, porque no sois de mis ovejas,
como os he dicho. 27 Mis ovejas oyen mi voz, y yo las conozco,
y me siguen; 28 Y yo les doy vida eterna y no perecerán para siempre,
ni nadie las arrebatará de mi mano.
~ Juan 10

My sheep hear My voice,
and I know them,
and they follow Me.
and I give them eternal life,
and they shall never perish;
neither shall anyone
snatch them out of My hand....
~ Jesus said that...

Luke

THEN HE SAID to the disciples,
"It is impossible that no offenses should come,
but woe to him through whom they do come!
It would be better for him
if a millstone were hung around his neck,
and he were thrown into the sea,
than that he should offend one of these little ones.
Take heed to yourselves. If your brother sins against you,
rebuke him;
and if he repents, forgive him. And if he sins against you
seven times in a day, and seven times in a day returns to you,
saying, 'I repent,' you shall forgive him."

~ Luke 17:1–4

لوقا 1:17-4

العثَراتُ وَالمُسامَحَة

17 وقالَ يَسُوعُ لِتَلاميذِهِ: «لا مَفَرَّ مِنْ حُدُوثِ العَثَراتِ، لَكِنْ وَيْلٌ لِذَلِكَ الإنسانِ الَّذِي تَأْتِي العَثَراتُ بِسَبَبِهِ! 2 سَيَكُونُ أفضَلَ لَهُ لَوْ أنَّ حَجَرَ الرَّحَى وُضِعَ حَوْلَ رَقَبَتِهِ، وَأُلْقِيَ بِهِ فِي البَحرِ، مِنْ أنْ يُوقِعَ أحَدَ هَؤُلاءِ الصِّغارِ فِي الخَطِيَّةِ. 3 فانتَبِهُوا لأنْفُسِكُمْ!

«إذا أساءَ أخُوكَ، فَوَبِّخْهُ، وَإذا اعتَذَرَ سامِحْهُ. 4 وَإذا أخطَأ إلَيكَ سَبعَ مَرّاتٍ فِي يَومٍ واحِدٍ، وَعادَ إلَيكَ سَبعَ مَرّاتٍ مُعتَذِراً، فسامِحْهُ.»

Y A SUS discípulos dice: Imposible es que no vengan escándalos; mas ¡ay de aquél por quien vienen! 2 Mejor le fuera, si le pusiesen al cuello una piedra de molino, y le lanzasen en el mar, que escandalizar á uno de estos pequeñitos. 3 Mirad por vosotros: si pecare contra ti tu hermano, repréndele; y si se arrepintiere, perdónale. 4 Y si siete veces al día pecare contra ti, y siete veces al día se volviere á ti, diciendo, pésame, perdónale.

~ Lucas 17

...woe to him
through whom they [offences*] do come!
It would be better for him
if a millstone were hung around his neck,
and he were thrown into the sea,
than that he should offend
one of these little ones.
~ Jesus said that...

*snare (figuratively, cause of displeasure or sin)

Matthew

ENTER BY THE narrow gate;
for wide is the gate and broad is the way
that leads to destruction,
and there are many who go in by it. Because narrow is the gate
and difficult is the way which leads to life,
and there are few who find it.
~ Matthew 7:13–14

متى 13:7-14

طَريقُ السَّماءِ وَطَريقُ الجَحيم

13 »ادخُلُوا مِنَ البابِ الضَّيِّقِ، الَّذي يُؤَدّي إلى السَّماءِ. لأنَّ البابَ الَّذي يُؤَدّي إلى الهلاكِ واسِعٌ، وَالطَّريقُ إلَيهِ سَهلٌ، وَكَثِيرُونَ يَدخُلُونَهُ. 14 أمّا البابُ الَّذي يُؤَدّي إلى الحَياةِ فَضَيِّقٌ جِدّاً، وَالطَّريقُ إلَيهِ مَليءٌ بِالصُّعُوباتِ، وَقَليلُونَ فَقَط هُم مَن يَجِدُونَ هَذا الطَّريقَ.

13 Entrad por la puerta estrecha: porque ancha es la puerta,
y espacioso el camino que lleva á perdición,
y muchos son los que entran por ella.
14 Porque estrecha es la puerta,
y angosto el camino que lleva á la vida, y
pocos son los que la hallan.
~ Mateo 7

...narrow is the gate
 and difficult is the way
  which leads to life,
 and there are few who find it.

~ Jesus said that...

Revelation & Matthew

AND BEHOLD, I am coming quickly,
and My reward is with Me,
to give to every one according to his work.
I am the Alpha and the Omega,
the Beginning and the End,
the First and the Last.
~ Revelation 22:12–13

Take heed, watch and pray;
for you do not know when the time is.
~ Matthew 13:33

يوحنا رؤيا 12:22-13

12 «ها أنا قادِمٌ سَريعاً، وَمَعِي الأُجرَةَ لِكَي أُجازِيَ كُلَّ واحِدٍ حَسَبَ أعمالِهِ. 13 أنا هُوَ الألِفُ والياءُ، [a] الأوَّلُ والآخِرُ، البِدايَةُ و النِّهايَةُ.

a. يوحنا رؤيا 22:13 *الألِف وَالياء*. في الأصل: «ألفا» و«أوميجا»، وهما الحرفان الأوّل وَالأخير من الحروف اليونانية، وَالمعنى: «البِداية وَالنهاية.»

متى 13:33

33 «احذَرُوا وَتَيَقَّظُوا، لِأنَّكُمْ لا تَعرِفُونَ مَتَى يَأتِي الوَقتُ.

12 Y he aquí, yo vengo presto, y mi galardón conmigo, para recompensar á cada uno según fuere su obra. 13 Yo soy Alpha y Omega, principio y fin, el primero y el postrero.

~ Apocalipsis 22

33 Mirad, velad y orad: porque no sabéis cuándo será el tiempo. ~ Mateo 13

And behold,
I am coming quickly,
and My reward is with Me,
to give to every one
according to his work.
I am the Alpha and the Omega,
the Beginning and the End,
the First and the Last.

~ Jesus said that...
and so much more.

Repent, for the kingdom of heaven is at hand.

توبوا ، لأن ملكوت السموات في متناول اليد.

Arrepiéntete, porque el reino de los cielos está cerca.

Did Jesus really say that?

Yes, and He said so much more.... As He (Jesus, "the Light of the world) pushed back the darkness, He—Jesus Himself said, "Repent...."

What does "repent" really mean?

To repent does not only mean that we are not sorry for things we did... for our sins, nor is repentance simply coming to see the Light. Repentance means having a radical heart and life change. Through repentance and surrendering to His Holy Spirit in obedience, we receive this Light in us. Jesus came to rock the world and turn religion upside down!

Matthew 4:16-17 (NKJV) records:

The people who sat in darkness have seen a great light,
And upon those who sat in the region and shadow of death
Light has dawned."
From that time Jesus began to preach and to say,
"Repent, for the kingdom of heaven is at hand."

Love God... Love People and Ride with Jesus....

~ Linda Foust Grajewski

Invitation

Who: God loves you. He gave His Son, Jesus Christ, to die on the cross for yOur sins.
~ John 3:16

What: Be "born again."
~ John 3:7

Receive God's Gift of Grace.
Through Jesus, God offers forgiveness of sins; assurance of eternal life; Heaven....
~ Ephesians 2:8-9

When:
Now... Today...
Behold, now is the accepted time; behold, now is the day of salvation.
~ 2 Corinthians 6:2b

Where: Wherever, Just as you are....
~ Romans 5:8

?: If you confess with yOur mouth the Lord Jesus and believe in your heart that God has raised Him [Jesus] from the dead, you will be saved.
~ Romans 10:9

رساله دعوة

من الذى: يوحنا 3:16

16 فَقَدْ أَحَبَّ اللهُ العالَمَ كَثِيراً، حَتَّى إِنَّهُ قَدَّمَ ابْنَهُ الوَحِيدَ، لِكَيْ لا يَهلِكَ كُلُّ مَنْ يُؤمِنُ بِهِ، بَلْ تَكُونُ لَهُ الحَياةُ الأبَدِيَّةُ.

ماذا: ~ جون 3: 7
أن "ولد من جديد".

أفسس 8:2-9

8 فبِالنِّعمَةِ أنْتُم مُخَلَّصُونَ، لأنَّكُم آمَنتُم، وَهَذا كُلُّهُ لا يَعتَمِدُ عليكُم، بَلْ هُوَ عَطِيَّةٌ مِنَ اللهِ. **9** ليسَ مُقابِلَ الأعمالِ لِئَلّا يَكُونَ هُناكَ مَجالٌ لِلافتِخارِ.

متى: 2 كورنثوس 6: 2 ب
الآن ... ليو ...
هوذا الان وقت مقبول.
هوذا الان يوم الخلاص.

أين: رومية 5:8
أينما، تماماً كما أنت ...

: رومية 10:9

9 إنْ أعلَنتَ بِشَفَتَيكَ، وَآمَنتَ بِقَلبِكَ، أنَّ يَسُوعَ رَبٌّ وَأنَّ اللهَ أقامَهُ مِنَ المَوتِ، خَلُصتَ.

Invitación

Quién: Dios te ama. Dio a su Hijo, Jesucristo, para morir en la cruz por tus pecados.
~ Juan 3:16

Qué: Ser "nacido de nuevo".
~ Juan 3:7

Recibe el don de la gracia de Dios. A través de Jesús, Dios ofrece perdón de pecados; seguridad de la vida eterna; Cielo….
~ Efesios 2:8--9

Cuándo: ahora … hoy …

He aquí, ahora es el tiempo aceptado; he aquí, ahora es el día de salvación.
~ 2 Corintios 6:2b

Dónde: donde sea, tal como eres …
~ Romanos 5:8

?: Si confiesas con tu boca al Señor Jesús y crees en tu corazón que Dios lo levantó de entre los muertos, serás salvo.
~ Romanos 10:9

www.ingramcontent.com/pod-product-compliance
Lightning Source LLC
Chambersburg PA
CBHW042121100526
44587CB00025B/4148